C000120197

HERE COMES THE SUN

RADIANT QUOTES TO WARM YOUR HEART AND BRIGHTEN YOUR DAY

summersdale

HERE COMES THE SUN

An Hachette UK Company
www.hachette.co.uk

Summersdale Publishers Ltd
Part of Octopus Publishing Group Limited
Carmelite House
50 Victoria Embankment
LONDON
EC4Y 0DZ
UK

www.summersdale.com

Printed and bound in the Czech Republic

ISBN: 978-1-80007-047-9

Substantial discounts on bulk quantities of Summersdale books are available to corporations, professional associations and other organizations. For details contact general enquiries: telephone: +44 (0) 1243 771107 or email: enquiries@summersdale.com.

TO..

FROM..

IF YOU HAVE
GOOD THOUGHTS
THEY WILL SHINE OUT OF
YOUR FACE LIKE SUNBEAMS
AND YOU WILL ALWAYS
LOOK LOVELY.

Roald Dahl

Optimism is a happiness magnet. If you stay positive, good things and good people will be drawn to you.

MARY LOU RETTON

FIND ECSTASY IN LIFE; THE MERE SENSE OF LIVING IS JOY ENOUGH.

Emily Dickinson

EVERY

MOMENT

HAS ITS

PLEASURES

AND ITS

HOPE.

JANE AUSTEN

NO MATTER HOW DARK THE SKIES MAY BE, *the sun is shining* **SOMEWHERE AND WILL EVENTUALLY COME** *smiling through.*

P. G. WODEHOUSE

THERE WAS NEVER A NIGHT OR A PROBLEM THAT COULD DEFEAT SUNRISE OR HOPE.

BERNARD WILLIAMS

Life isn't about waiting
for the storm to pass;
it's about learning to
dance in the rain.

ANONYMOUS

SEIZE EVERY
OPPORTUNITY
TO DANCE, TO
LAUGH AND TO
SPREAD JOY

The universe is
full of magical
things patiently
waiting for our wits
to grow sharper.

EDEN PHILLPOTTS

JOY IS WHAT HAPPENS TO US WHEN WE ALLOW OURSELVES TO RECOGNIZE HOW GOOD THINGS REALLY ARE.

MARIANNE WILLIAMSON

TOGETHER WE CAN ENSURE THAT TOMORROW WILL BE A GOOD DAY.

Captain Sir Tom Moore

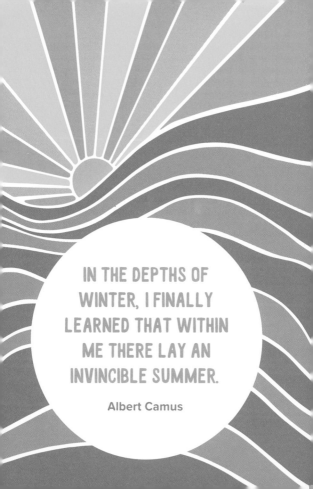

IN THE DEPTHS OF
WINTER, I FINALLY
LEARNED THAT WITHIN
ME THERE LAY AN
INVINCIBLE SUMMER.

Albert Camus

One joy
scatters a
hundred griefs.

CHINESE PROVERB

GOOD
VIBES
ONLY

WHEN LIFE LOOKS
LIKE IT'S ━━━━

FALLING
APART,

━ IT MAY JUST BE

FALLING
IN PLACE.

BEVERLY SOLOMON

THE FORMULA OF
happiness
and success
IS JUST BEING
ACTUALLY YOURSELF,
in the most vivid
possible way
YOU CAN.

MERYL STREEP

GIVE LIGHT, AND THE DARKNESS WILL DISAPPEAR OF ITSELF.

DESIDERIUS ERASMUS

Turn your face toward
the sun and the shadows
will fall behind you.

MĀORI PROVERB

EVERY MOMENT
IS AUSPICIOUS.
THERE IS ALWAYS
SOME MAGIC IN IT.

AMIT RAY

I don't think of all
the misery, but of
the beauty that
still remains.

ANNE FRANK

BRIGHTER DAYS ARE COMING

I DO NOT
BELIEVE THAT
ANY DARKNESS
WILL ENDURE.

J. R. R. Tolkien

THAT IS ONE GOOD
THING ABOUT THIS
WORLD... THERE ARE
ALWAYS SURE TO BE
MORE SPRINGS.

L. M. Montgomery

Every day brings
a chance for
you to draw in
a breath, kick
off your shoes...
and dance.

OPRAH WINFREY

THERE ARE TWO WAYS
OF SPREADING LIGHT:
TO BE THE CANDLE,
OR THE MIRROR THAT
REFLECTS IT.

Edith Wharton

SING
LIKE THE BIRDS —
SING
— NOT WORRYING ABOUT
WHO HEARS OR WHAT —
THEY THINK.

RUMI

THERE
ARE ALWAYS
flowers
FOR THOSE WHO
want to see them.

HENRI MATISSE

DON'T
LET ANYONE
DULL YOUR
SPARKLE

If you go out and make
some good things happen,
you will fill the world
with hope, you will fill
yourself with hope.

BARACK OBAMA

LIFE SHRINKS OR EXPANDS ACCORDING TO ONE'S COURAGE.

ANAÏS NIN

Some days there
won't be a song
in your heart.
Sing anyway.

EMORY AUSTIN

THE WAY I SEE IT, IF YOU WANT THE RAINBOW, YOU GOTTA PUT UP WITH THE RAIN.

DOLLY PARTON

HAPPINESS BLOOMS FROM WITHIN

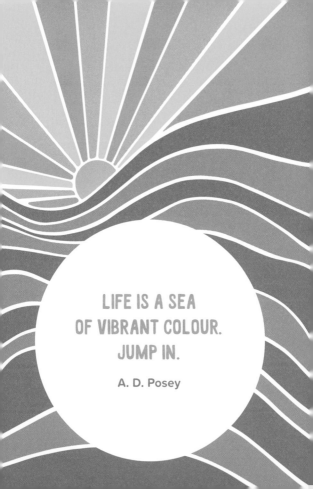

LIFE IS A SEA
OF VIBRANT COLOUR.
JUMP IN.

A. D. Posey

You've got
to get up every
morning with
determination
if you're going
to go to bed with
satisfaction.

GEORGE LORIMER

LIFE IS EITHER
A DARING ADVENTURE
OR NOTHING.

Helen Keller

CHANGE YOUR —

THOUGHTS

AND YOU CHANGE YOUR

WORLD.

NORMAN VINCENT PEALE

Hope
IS NOT SOMETHING
THAT YOU HAVE.
HOPE IS SOMETHING
THAT YOU
create,
WITH YOUR
actions.

ALEXANDRIA OCASIO-CORTEZ

FOLLOWING
THE BEND IN
THE RIVER AND
STAYING ON
YOUR OWN PATH
MEANS THAT
YOU ARE ON THE
RIGHT TRACK.

EARTHA KITT

The sun himself is
weak when he first rises,
and gathers strength and
courage as the day gets on.

CHARLES DICKENS

ONE STEP AT
A TIME, I GET TO
MAKE POSITIVE
CHOICES TO FULFIL
MY DREAMS.

DEENA KASTOR

Life is a journey
- enjoy the ride

TELL ME,
WHAT IS IT
YOU PLAN TO
DO WITH YOUR
ONE WILD AND
PRECIOUS
LIFE?

MARY OLIVER

BEAUTY IS EVERYWHERE – YOU ONLY HAVE TO LOOK TO SEE IT.

Bob Ross

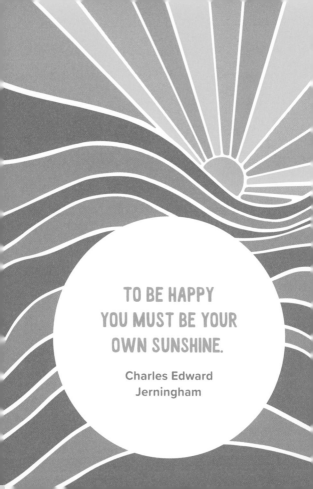

TO BE HAPPY
YOU MUST BE YOUR
OWN SUNSHINE.

Charles Edward
Jerningham

I'm not afraid of storms, for I'm learning how to sail my ship.

LOUISA MAY ALCOTT

OPPORTUNITY DANCES WITH THOSE WHO ARE ALREADY ON THE DANCE FLOOR.

H. Jackson Brown Jr

HAPPINESS OFTEN —

SNEAKS

— IN THROUGH A DOOR
YOU DIDN'T KNOW —
— YOU LEFT

OPEN.

JOHN BARRYMORE

ONE SMALL
positive thought
CAN CHANGE YOUR
whole day.

ZIG ZIGLAR

YOU'RE THE BLACKSMITH OF YOUR OWN HAPPINESS.

SWEDISH PROVERB

For every minute
you are angry you
lose 60 seconds
of happiness.

RALPH WALDO EMERSON

TODAY,
I CHOOSE
HAPPINESS

Tomorrow is the first day of the rest of our lives.

TERRY PRATCHETT

WITH THE NEW DAY COMES NEW STRENGTH AND NEW THOUGHTS.

ELEANOR ROOSEVELT

LIFE IS A FAIRY TALE. LIVE IT WITH WONDER AND AMAZEMENT.

Welwyn Wilton Katz

DO WHAT
MAKES YOUR
SOUL SHINE

When you come
to a roadblock,
take a detour.

MARY KAY ASH

PERHAPS OUR EYES
NEED TO BE WASHED BY
OUR TEARS ONCE IN
A WHILE, SO THAT WE
CAN SEE LIFE WITH A
CLEARER VIEW AGAIN.

Anonymous

DON'T

LET ANYONE

STEAL

YA JOY!

MISSY ELLIOTT

IT'S ALL RIGHT
TO HAVE
butterflies
IN YOUR STOMACH.
JUST GET THEM TO
fly in formation.

ROB GILBERT

FEAR NEVER BUILDS THE FUTURE, BUT HOPE DOES.

JOE BIDEN

I believe if you
put out positive
vibes to everybody,
that's all you're
going to get back.

KESHA

LOOK FOR THE POSITIVES IN EVERY SITUATION

We must
accept finite
disappointment,
but never lose
infinite hope.

MARTIN LUTHER KING JR

FOLLOW YOUR PASSION, FOLLOW YOUR HEART, AND THE THINGS YOU NEED WILL COME.

ELIZABETH TAYLOR

WHAT A WONDERFUL LIFE I'VE HAD! I ONLY WISH I'D REALIZED IT SOONER.

Colette

REMEMBER,
HOPE IS A GOOD THING,
MAYBE THE BEST OF
THINGS, AND NO GOOD
THING EVER DIES.

Stephen King

A generous heart, kind speech and a life of service and compassion are the things that renew humanity.

BUDDHIST PROVERB

IT TAKES A LOT OF HARD WORK TO REMAIN POSITIVE, BUT POSITIVITY ALWAYS PAYS OFF.

RuPaul

— CELEBRATE EVERY

WIN,

NO MATTER HOW —

SMALL

HOWEVER BAD LIFE
MAY SEEM, THERE IS
always something
YOU CAN DO AND
succeed at.
WHILE THERE'S LIFE,
there is hope.

STEPHEN HAWKING

I KNOW THE SUN
WILL RISE IN
THE MORNING,
THAT THERE
IS A LIGHT AT
THE END OF
EVERY TUNNEL.

MICHAEL MORPURGO

The world is
always open, waiting
to be discovered.

DEJAN STOJANOVIĆ

EVERY DAY BRINGS NEW CHOICES.

MARTHA BECK

Joy does not simply
happen to us. We have
to choose joy and keep
choosing it every day.

HENRI NOUWEN

HAPPINESS HELD IS THE SEED; HAPPINESS SHARED IS THE FLOWER.

JOHN HARRIGAN

**TODAY'S
TO-DO LIST:**

**DREAM
BELIEVE
BE HAPPY**

EVERY DAY MAY
NOT BE GOOD... BUT
THERE'S SOMETHING
GOOD IN EVERY DAY.

Alice Morse Earle

I take the best, get rid of the rest, and move on, realizing that you can make a choice to take the good.

BROOKE SHIELDS

LIFE IS THE DANCER AND YOU ARE THE DANCE.

Eckhart Tolle

YOUR STRUGGLES DEVELOP YOUR STRENGTHS.

ARNOLD SCHWARZENEGGER

LOOK AT THE

sunny side

OF EVERYTHING
AND MAKE YOUR

optimism

COME TRUE.

CHRISTIAN D. LARSON

DON'T EVER MAKE DECISIONS BASED ON FEAR. MAKE DECISIONS BASED ON HOPE AND POSSIBILITY.

MICHELLE OBAMA

Always leave enough time
in your life to do something
that makes you happy,
satisfied, even joyous.

PAUL HAWKEN

START
EACH DAY
WITH
A SMILE

You are ready
and able to do
beautiful things
in this world.

JIM CARREY

TRY TO BE A RAINBOW IN SOMEONE'S CLOUD.

MAYA ANGELOU

IF YOU SPEND
YOUR WHOLE LIFE
WAITING FOR THE
STORM, YOU'LL
NEVER ENJOY
THE SUNSHINE.

Morris West

HAPPINESS...
NOT IN ANOTHER
PLACE, BUT THIS PLACE...
NOT FOR ANOTHER HOUR,
BUT THIS HOUR.

Walt Whitman

We can complain because rose bushes have thorns or we can rejoice because thorn bushes have roses.

ANONYMOUS

WHEN YOU FOCUS
ON THE GOOD,
THE GOOD GETS
EVEN BETTER

IT IS NOT
HOW MUCH
WE HAVE,
BUT HOW MUCH WE
ENJOY,
THAT MAKES
HAPPINESS.

CHARLES SPURGEON

Good things
COME TO PEOPLE
WHO WAIT, BUT
better things
COME TO THOSE
WHO GO OUT AND
get them.

ANONYMOUS

LIFE IS TOUGH; AND IF YOU HAVE THE ABILITY TO LAUGH AT IT, YOU HAVE THE ABILITY TO ENJOY IT.

SALMA HAYEK

Happiness is letting go of what you think your life is supposed to look like and celebrating it for everything that it is.

MANDY HALE

SOME PEOPLE
GO TO PRIESTS;
OTHERS TO POETRY;
I TO MY FRIENDS.

VIRGINIA WOOLF

May you live
every day of
your life.

JONATHAN SWIFT

SQUEEZE THE DAY!

LET US BE
GRATEFUL TO THE
PEOPLE WHO MAKE US
HAPPY; THEY ARE THE
CHARMING GARDENERS
WHO MAKE OUR
SOULS BLOSSOM.

Marcel Proust

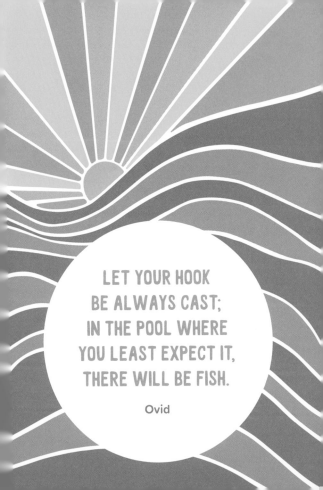

LET YOUR HOOK
BE ALWAYS CAST;
IN THE POOL WHERE
YOU LEAST EXPECT IT,
THERE WILL BE FISH.

Ovid

I can't change the direction of the wind, but I can adjust my sails to always reach my destination.

JIMMY DEAN

IF YOU LOVE LIFE, LIFE WILL LOVE YOU BACK.

Arthur Rubinstein

HOW WONDERFUL IT
IS THAT

NOBODY

NEED WAIT A SINGLE
MOMENT BEFORE
STARTING TO

IMPROVE

THE WORLD.

ANNE FRANK

I WAKE UP
EVERY MORNING
believing
TODAY IS
GOING TO BE
better
THAN YESTERDAY.

WILL SMITH

TODAY'S A
GREAT DAY
TO HAVE A
GREAT DAY

Positive anything
is better than
negative nothing.

ELBERT HUBBARD

TURN YOUR HAPPINESS UP TO 11

You can cut all
the flowers but you
cannot keep spring
from coming.

PABLO NERUDA

THERE'S ALWAYS TOMORROW AND IT ALWAYS GETS BETTER!

ARIANA GRANDE

FEELINGS ARE
MUCH LIKE WAVES,
WE CAN'T STOP THEM
FROM COMING, BUT
WE CAN CHOOSE
WHICH ONES TO SURF.

Jonatan Mårtensson

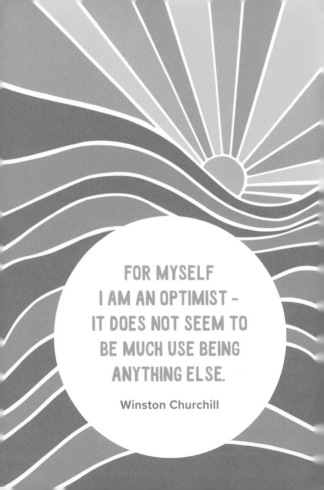

FOR MYSELF
I AM AN OPTIMIST –
IT DOES NOT SEEM TO
BE MUCH USE BEING
ANYTHING ELSE.

Winston Churchill

Learn to enjoy every minute of your life. Be happy now. Don't wait for something outside of yourself to make you happy in the future.

EARL NIGHTINGALE

IT'S NEVER TOO LATE – NEVER TOO LATE TO START OVER, NEVER TOO LATE TO BE HAPPY.

Jane Fonda

STAY CLOSE
— TO ANYTHING
THAT MAKES YOU
GLAD
YOU ARE —
ALIVE.

HAFEZ

IT IS ALWAYS THE

simple

THAT PRODUCES THE

marvellous.

AMELIA BARR

TIME IS A GREAT RESTORER, AND CHANGES SURELY THE GREATEST SORROW INTO A PLEASING MEMORY.

MARY SEACOLE

You're going to be OK.
Better than OK.
You're going to be great.

REESE WITHERSPOON

ACCENTUATE THE POSITIVE, NOT THE NEGATIVE.

BETTY WHITE

Positivity
is your
Superpower

LOVE WILL FIND A WAY THROUGH PATHS WHERE WOLVES FEAR TO PREY.

LORD BYRON

HOPE IS BEING
ABLE TO SEE THAT
THERE IS LIGHT
DESPITE ALL OF
THE DARKNESS.

Desmond Tutu

THOSE WHO
BRING SUNSHINE INTO
THE LIVES OF OTHERS
CANNOT KEEP IT
FROM THEMSELVES.

J. M. Barrie

Hope is the thing
with feathers
That perches
in the soul,
And sings the
tune without
the words,
And never
stops at all.

EMILY DICKINSON

WHY NOT JUST LIVE IN THE MOMENT, ESPECIALLY IF IT HAS A GOOD BEAT?

Goldie Hawn

PERPETUAL **OPTIMISM...** IS A **FORCE** MULTIPLIER.

THERE IS

something

GOOD IN

every day

EVERYTHING THAT IS DONE IN THE WORLD IS DONE BY HOPE.

MARTIN LUTHER

Nothing is worth more
than laughter. It is strength
to laugh and to abandon
oneself, to be light.

FRIDA KAHLO

FILL
YOUR LIFE
WITH THINGS
THAT BRING
YOU JOY

Extraordinary things
are always hiding
in places people
never think to look.

JODI PICOULT

TOUGH TIMES NEVER LAST, BUT TOUGH PEOPLE DO!

ROBERT H. SCHULLER

OPTIMISM IS THE
FAITH THAT LEADS
TO ACHIEVEMENT.
NOTHING CAN BE
DONE WITHOUT HOPE
AND CONFIDENCE.

Helen Keller

ISN'T IT NICE TO
THINK THAT TOMORROW
IS A NEW DAY WITH NO
MISTAKES IN IT YET?

L. M. Montgomery

Happiness is
a perfume you
cannot pour on
others without
getting a few
drops on yourself.

RALPH WALDO EMERSON

ESSENTIALS TO HAPPINESS IN THIS LIFE ARE SOMETHING TO DO, SOMETHING TO LOVE, AND SOMETHING TO HOPE FOR.

Héctor García

THE PAST IS
GONE.
TODAY IS
FULL OF
POSSIBILITIES.

KAREN CASEY

IF YOU'RE FEELING LOW,
don't despair.
THE SUN HAS A
sinking spell
EVERY NIGHT,
BUT IT COMES BACK UP
every morning.

DOLLY PARTON

IF WE
BELIEVE THAT
TOMORROW WILL
BE BETTER,
WE CAN BEAR
A HARDSHIP
TODAY.

THÍCH NHÁT HANH

At every moment
in our life we have
the opportunity
to choose joy.

HENRI NOUWEN

ALWAYS
LOOK ON THE
BRIGHT SIDE

The pain passes but the beauty remains.

PIERRE-AUGUSTE RENOIR

WHATEVER
YOU'RE GOING
THROUGH IN
YOUR LIFE,
DON'T EVER
GIVE UP.

MARIAH CAREY

THE SUN
IS NEW
EACH DAY.

Heraclitus

IF YOU'RE
WALKING DOWN THE
RIGHT PATH AND YOU'RE
WILLING TO KEEP WALKING,
EVENTUALLY YOU'LL
MAKE PROGRESS.

Barack Obama

Listen.
Pay attention.
Treasure every
moment.

OPRAH WINFREY

IF YOU TRULY POUR
YOUR HEART INTO
WHAT YOU BELIEVE IN...
AMAZING THINGS CAN
AND WILL HAPPEN.

Emma Watson

THE MOST
IMPORTANT
THING IS TO
ENJOY YOUR
LIFE – TO BE
HAPPY – IT'S
ALL THAT
MATTERS.

AUDREY HEPBURN

THERE ARE
SO MANY
great things

IN LIFE;
WHY DWELL ON
negativity?

ZENDAYA

THIS IS A WONDERFUL DAY. I'VE NEVER SEEN THIS ONE BEFORE.

MAYA ANGELOU

Part of being optimistic is keeping one's head pointed toward the sun, one's feet moving forward.

NELSON MANDELA

IF YOU SMILE, THINGS WILL WORK OUT.

SERENA WILLIAMS

When it's dark,
look for stars

IF WINTER COMES, CAN SPRING BE FAR BEHIND?

PERCY BYSSHE SHELLEY

WHEREVER YOU GO, NO MATTER WHAT THE WEATHER, ALWAYS BRING YOUR OWN SUNSHINE.

Anthony J. D'Angelo

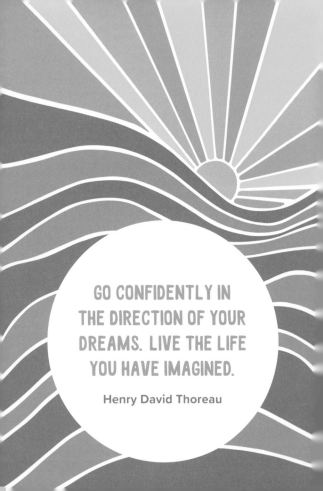

GO CONFIDENTLY IN
THE DIRECTION OF YOUR
DREAMS. LIVE THE LIFE
YOU HAVE IMAGINED.

Henry David Thoreau

Even the
darkest night
will end and the
sun will rise.

VICTOR HUGO

Have you enjoyed this book?
If so, find us on Facebook at Summersdale
Publishers, on Twitter at @Summersdale and
on Instagram at @summersdalebooks and
get in touch. We'd love to hear from you!

www.summersdale.com

Image credits

Cover image and sun on pp.1, 4, 10, 15, 21, 26, 32,
37, 43, 48, 54, 59, 65, 70, 76, 81, 87, 92, 98,
103, 109, 114, 120, 125, 131, 136, 142, 147, 153,
158 © Designs World/Shutterstock.com